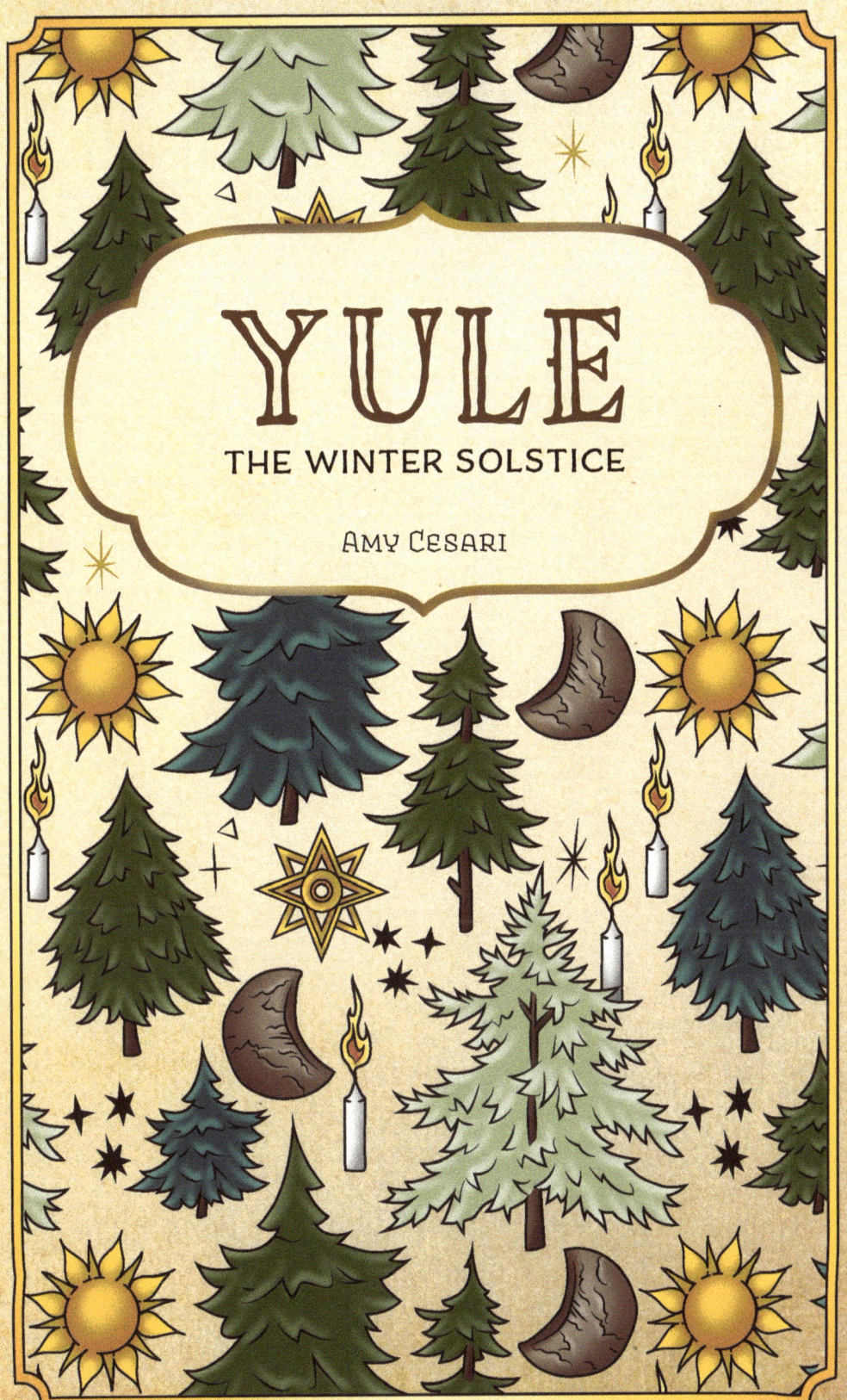

Be a fire-safe witch!

- Lots of space above and around the flame.
- Candle is on a fire-safe dish.
- Never leave flames unattended.

COPYRIGHT & GENERAL DISCLAIMER:
YULE THE WINTER SOLSTICE
ALL TEXT AND IMAGES © 2017-2025 BOOK OF SHADOWS LLC, AMY CESARI

THIS BOOK DOES NOT CONTAIN MEDICAL ADVICE AND DOES NOT INTEND TO TREAT OR DIAGNOSE MEDICAL OR HEALTH ISSUES. ALWAYS SEEK PROFESSIONAL MEDICAL TREATMENT. AND DON'T EAT OR USE PLANTS IF YOU DON'T KNOW WHAT THEY ARE.

ALL RIGHTS RESERVED. For personal use only. No parts of this book may be reproduced, copied, or transmitted in any form, by any means, including photocopying, recording, or other electronic or mechanical methods, without the prior written permission of the author, except in the case of brief quotations for critical reviews and certain other noncommercial uses permitted by copyright law. **DISCLAIMER OF LIABILITY:** This book is for informational and entertainment purposes only and is not intended as a substitute for medical, financial, spiritual, or life advice of any kind. Like any craft involving flames, the power of your mind unhinged, eating plants and herbs, and the unyielding forces of the universe, Witchcraft poses some inherent risk. The author and publisher are not liable or responsible for any outcome of magical spells performed from this book or otherwise. Readers agree to cast spells, work with fire, ingest herbs, soak in bath salts, light candles and incense, channel deities, use spirit boards, and perform any and all other magical practices at their own risk. The images in this book are for decorative purposes—they are not realistic guides for arranging flame-based altars. Always place a fireproof dish beneath candles & incense. Leave clearance above & around flames. Do not place flammable objects near flames and never leave flaming things or incense unattended. Readers of this book take full responsibility when using fire. Readers accept full personal risk and responsibility for the outcome, consequence, and magic of any spells they cast. This book is not for children. And so it shall be.

This Book Belongs To:

What is Yule?

Yule and the Winter Solstice are celebrations of the longest night (and shortest day) of the year. Yule is the turning point where the days will begin to lengthen again—a cause for celebration of the sun.

The sun symbolizes hope, renewal, and the promise of brighter days ahead. It also represents the light within yourself, even during the darkest times, and the quiet wisdom of reflection and introspection.

The darkness of Yule is a powerful time to honor the cycles of rest and renewal, embracing the quiet strength that comes from turning inward and reconnecting with your inner light.

Yule is celebrated approximately December 21 in the northern hemisphere, which corresponds seasonally to June 21 in the southern hemisphere of Earth.

The Wheel of the Year
- and the -
Phases of the Moon

The seasons or the "Wheel of the Year" relate to the cycles, tilt, and planetary motion right here on Earth. Ancient Celts celebrated these seasonal shifts and used them for magic and ritual, as noted on the chart above. The moon shares a shorter, corresponding cycle, which completes in 28 days instead of 365 days in a year.

SOUTHERN HEMISPHERE SEASONS: If you're on the "southern" half of the Earth, like in Australia, the seasonal shifts are opposite. So you'll feel the energy of the summer solstice (corresponding to the full moon) in December instead of June.

A Note About the Cross-Quarter Dates: The dates for the two solstices and two equinoxes each year—Ostara, Litha, Mabon, and Yule—are calculated astronomically from the position of the Earth to the sun. The "cross-quarter" festivals, which are the points between —Imbolc, Beltane, Lughnasadh, and Samhain—are often celebrated on "fixed" dates instead of the actual midpoints. It's more common to celebrate on "fixed festival dates." Choose either date or any time in between for your own festivities or ritual. 'Tis the season for magic.

HISTORY
OF YULE
& THE WINTER SOLSTICE

For thousands of years, people have honored the winter solstice with rituals, traditions, and legends connecting us to the power of the earth, the divine, the cosmos, and the ever-turning cycles of nature.

People of ancient times lived closely with the cycles of nature in order to survive.

Imagine the dark of winter, where crops didn't grow, the air was frigid, and hunting was scarce. People rationed supplies and food gathered in warmer days. The winter was dangerous and likely felt endless.

Yule is a time where darkness is at its peak. But faith in the cycles of the sun and the inevitable return of the light spark a sense of reverence and hope. Yule offers a space to pause and reflect on both life and death.

Modern celebrations of Yule come from a collection of ancient practices, primarily rooted in various European pagan and pre-Christian traditions.

The word "Yule" has multiple origins from several languages, notably Old English, Old Norse, and possibly Germanic etymology.

The word "solstice" comes from the Latin word "solstitium," meaning "Sun stands still"—as the sun sets at approximately the same point for six days at the solstices.

Many of the historic pagan customs of Yule and the winter solstice center around fire, light, feasting, singing, and raising spirits in the darkness.

Some ancient traditions also celebrated and honored deities at the winter solstice. These rituals and prayers ensured abundant supplies and a prosperous harvest ahead. To this day, these customs live on and remind us that the sun will return, and spring will come again.

HISTORY
OF YULE
& THE WINTER SOLSTICE

There is far more history and nuance to the fascinating folklore and legends of the winter solstice than can fit in the scope of this book.

Seek out more on the cultures that interest you. You'll be surprised and delighted when you discover more about the traditions that were carried forward into the modern world, and there are many fascinating examples.

Ancient Celtic and Druid traditions called the winter solstice "Alban Arthan," weaving their celebrations into the lore of King Arthur and the return of light or hope.

In Norse mythology, you might witness "the Wild Hunt" on the winter solstice. The Wild Hunt is a procession of spirits and otherworldly beings led by the God Odin. They ride through the sky in search of the lost sun, representing the eternal struggle between light and dark.

In ancient Egypt, the solstice was linked to the rebirth of the sun god, Ra. The Great Pyramids align with the sun's rising and setting and represent Ra's journey across the sky. During the solstice, the sun's rays symbolize the return of life, hope, and warmth despite the darkness of winter.

Native American traditions also revere the winter solstice as a time of honoring the Earth and its cycles. Ceremonies are held for blessings of renewal, prosperity, and peace. These rituals align with the solstice as a time for reflection, rest, and the coming return of the sun, signaling new beginnings and growth.

Although each culture and tradition has their own remarkable and distinct ways of celebrating, the common thread is a deep reverence for the natural cycles of light and dark and the recognition of the sun's essential role in maintaining life and balance on Earth.

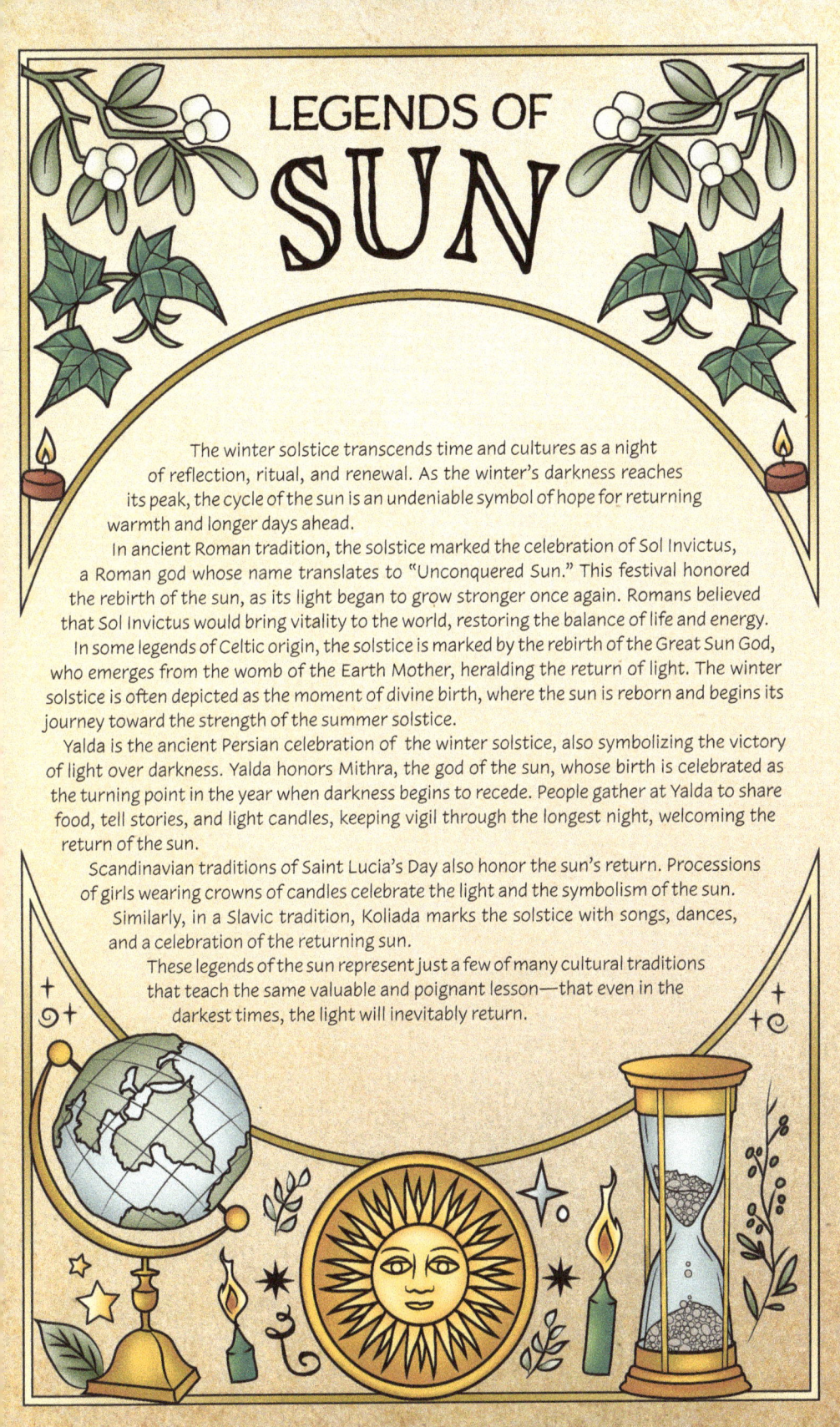

LEGENDS OF SUN

The winter solstice transcends time and cultures as a night of reflection, ritual, and renewal. As the winter's darkness reaches its peak, the cycle of the sun is an undeniable symbol of hope for returning warmth and longer days ahead.

In ancient Roman tradition, the solstice marked the celebration of Sol Invictus, a Roman god whose name translates to "Unconquered Sun." This festival honored the rebirth of the sun, as its light began to grow stronger once again. Romans believed that Sol Invictus would bring vitality to the world, restoring the balance of life and energy.

In some legends of Celtic origin, the solstice is marked by the rebirth of the Great Sun God, who emerges from the womb of the Earth Mother, heralding the return of light. The winter solstice is often depicted as the moment of divine birth, where the sun is reborn and begins its journey toward the strength of the summer solstice.

Yalda is the ancient Persian celebration of the winter solstice, also symbolizing the victory of light over darkness. Yalda honors Mithra, the god of the sun, whose birth is celebrated as the turning point in the year when darkness begins to recede. People gather at Yalda to share food, tell stories, and light candles, keeping vigil through the longest night, welcoming the return of the sun.

Scandinavian traditions of Saint Lucia's Day also honor the sun's return. Processions of girls wearing crowns of candles celebrate the light and the symbolism of the sun.

Similarly, in a Slavic tradition, Koliada marks the solstice with songs, dances, and a celebration of the returning sun.

These legends of the sun represent just a few of many cultural traditions that teach the same valuable and poignant lesson—that even in the darkest times, the light will inevitably return.

LEGENDS
OF THE LONGEST NIGHT

The night of the winter solstice may seem to stretch endlessly before the first glimmer of the sunrise appears on the horizon.

According to legends, this darkness is not seen as a defeat, but as a necessary part of the eternal dance between light and dark.

In Norse mythology, solstice legends tell of the struggle between the gods and the forces of chaos. The long night is a time when the world is engulfed by darkness as the sun must rest, gathering strength for its inevitable return.

But the great wolf Skoll chases the sun, trying to devour it in its weakened form. This symbolizes the relentless pull of darkness that seeks to overtake the light.

In Greek mythology, the solstice is linked to the god Hades, ruler of the underworld. In this legend, the longest night represents a descent into darkness, a time when the earth is still and silent. Yet it is also the time when Demeter, goddess of the harvest, begins her search for her daughter Persephone, who spends the dark half of the year in the underworld.

Persephone's return in spring symbolizes the restoration of balance, where darkness gives way to light once again.

In Christian tradition, the solstice is the moment when Christ, the "light of the world and the Son of God" is born. Sound familiar? Christ's story is a retelling of this ageless tale, the birth of a great hope in a time of darkness.

Legends of the longest night remind us that darkness is not to be feared. It is a sacred time of rest, renewal, and reflection, holding within it the promise of the return of light and brighter days ahead.

In pitch darkness, burn frankincense and myrrh to connect to the divine. Light a candle and make a wish from the depths of your soul.

LEGENDS OF SPIRITS

In some traditions, the solstice is not just a celebration of the returning sun, but also a time when the veil between worlds is thin, and spirits roam the earth. These winter spirits can be dangerous, but they also embody the mysteries of transformation, renewal, and the forces of nature.

In Norse mythology, the Wild Hunt brings both foreboding and excitement. A sighting of the Wild Hunt may herald the return of the sun; however it can also be an omen of war, famine, or other dark events to come. As such, it must be respected. Scandinavian and Norse traditions also tell us of hose spirits like the Nisse and Tomte. They might help guard your home—if they are given proper respect. To honor them, leave out a bowl of porridge as a gift to avoid the spirits' tricks and encourage their favor.

In Slavic traditions, winter spirits are often depicted as mischievous, yet protective figures. One of these spirits is Morozko or "Father Frost." Morozko is known for his ability to freeze both the land and the hearts of humans, but he is also a harbinger of renewal.

In Native American traditions, winter spirits are often associated with animals. The wolf, bear, and owl are winter animal spirits that guide people through the colder months.

In European folklore, the Yule Goat brings both mischief and good fortune. The Yule Goat roams the countryside on the solstice, visiting homes to deliver gifts and blessings. However, the Yule Goat is also known for its playful nature, sometimes causing pranks and mishaps.

In Celtic traditions, winter spirits are closely tied to the Earth's deep rest. The Cailleach, a winter goddess, is a figure of both destruction and rebirth, as she blankets the land in frost to aid in the Earth's rest, and prepare it for the coming spring.

These winter spirits remind us that even in the danger of the coldest and darkest nights, there is a purpose and hope for magic, transformation, and life's renewal.

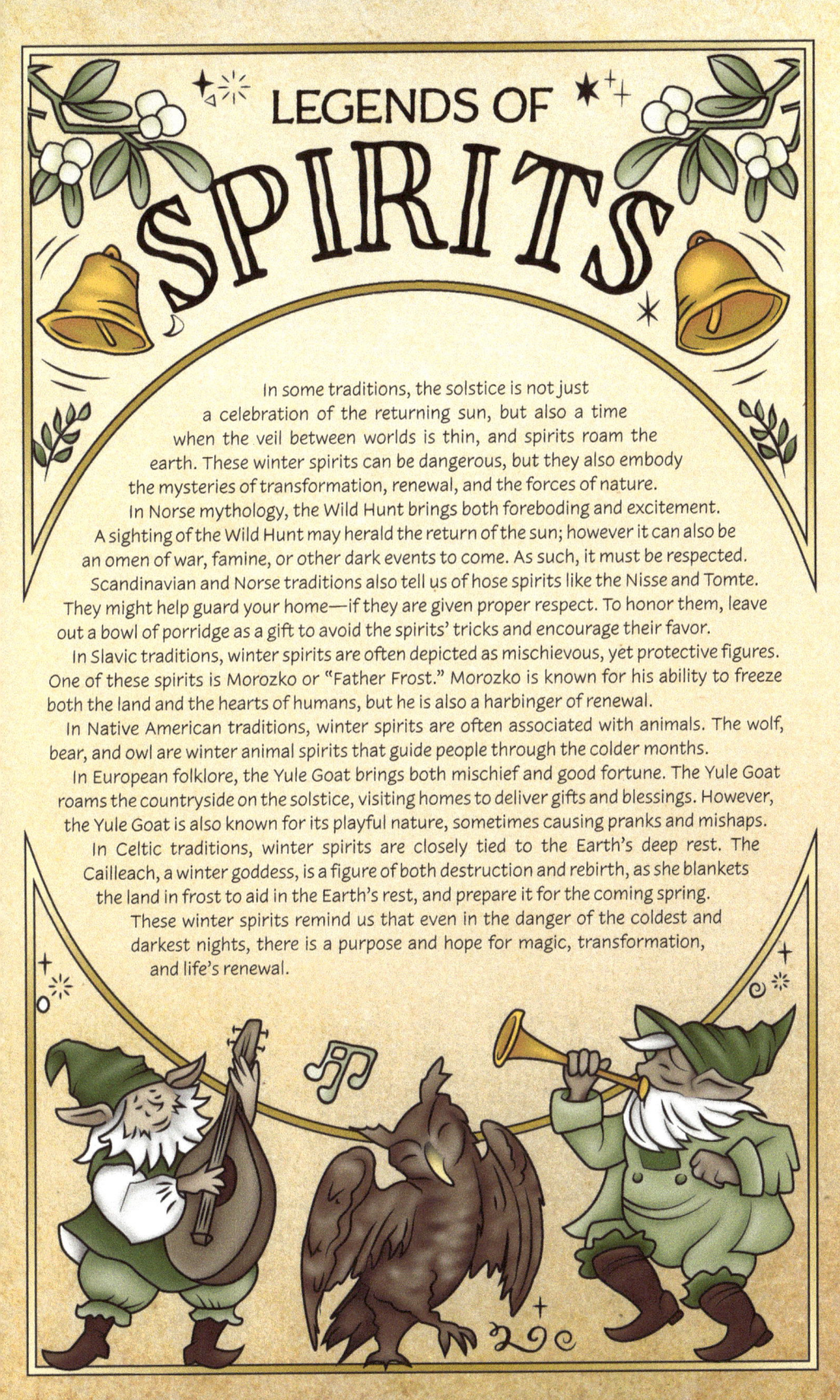

Ivy and evergreens symbolize the immortality of the soul.

Yew makes an powerful wand wood, but handle it with care. It's toxic!

Feel the magic of peace and acceptance. Decorate your home with herbs and evergreens to bring light and energy to yourself in the present.

Work with bloodstone and holly to feel peace in the present moment.

Mix a magical floor wash with water, a little white vinegar, a sprinkle of salt, and a few drops of pet-safe essential oil.

Yule Spells
Earth Element

Tidy
If your spirit feels low, clean up a little to reset the energetics of your space.

Decorate
Bring cheer to the darkness with homemade decorations.

Altar
Center your magic at a winter altar. It will bring light & energy to the winter.

Create
Winter is a lovely time to craft, cook, and write. Do things with your hands to recharge your spirit.

Ground
Connect to the energy of the earth to slowly & gently regain your power.

Read
Low on energy? Read or watch movies to enliven your imagination.

Candles signify light, hope, & possibility. Give them as a gift or treat yourself to a few.

Creating A Yule Altar
Centering Your Magical Focus and Intentions

Creating a seasonal altar is a powerful way to center your sabbat celebration.

An altar is a place to bring the spiritual into the material world—As Above, So Below. Altars speak to your subconscious in a way that's deeper than words or rational thought. They can help uncover feelings or powers within yourself that may be indescribable and will set the stage to inspire magic and ritual in life.

To create an altar that represents the energy of the winter solstice, collect a few items that evoke the essence of winter to you—herbs, crystals, animal symbols, deities, candles, scents, or things you've crafted or created.

Try asking yourself some reflective questions to spark ideas and inspiration. How do you want your winter to feel? If you're looking for cozy vibes, perhaps choose woodland creatures or warm scents like apples and cinnamon. If you've been missing family, friends, or departed loved ones, add photos, mementos, trinkets, and remembrances of those you love.

For a more balanced traditional altar, place statuary or representations of the "masculine" god and "feminine" goddess—these can be the Sun and Moon or deities of your choice or calling. Then add representations of the four elements, a bowl of water, candles for fire, salt or evergreens for earth, and incense or aromatic oils for the element of air.

But, of course, these are just ideas. While it's fine to look outward for inspiration, listen to the language of your soul and pick colors, scents, deities, and symbols that are uniquely yours.

Let your Yule altar be a place of power and reflection for the turning of the season, helping you harness the energies of winter, inspire your magical workings, and focus your energy.

Yule Herbcraft
Keeping Life and Light Alive in Winter

Even as the Earth rests in winter, there are signs of life if you look and listen closely. Craft with herbs and natural elements to cast creative spells with Earth's energy.

Evergreens are a potent symbol of Yule because they represent the undying life of nature. Use freshly-cut evergreens to create brooms, wreaths, and garlands. Tie them with colorful ribbons, bows, bells, charms, and painted dried acorns.

Festive garlands strung with popcorn, dried oranges, and cranberries are a classic way to enliven your Yule.

Pomanders are another classic adornment steeped in ritual and tradition. The repetitive process of sticking cloves in oranges will give you a few precious moments to clear your mind. Once completed, hang your pomander so its protective properties and scent can transform the energy of your home.

Wreaths are not just for doors, they're for soup, too. Create small herbal wreaths with sprigs of your favorite culinary herbs. Tie them with kitchen twine and toss them into your soup or stew. Breathe deeply as the scents fill your kitchen and soothe your soul.

If you've got the resources, making candles is always a worthwhile endeavor. Press or mix crushed herbs into the wax to add magical properties or anoint them with aromatic oils. Craft candles with bayberry wax for luck and prosperity or with beeswax for happiness, joy, and lighthearted energy.

And there's still powerful magic when you keep things simple. Fill potpourri bags with combinations of dried herbs, taking your time to smell them deeply, experiencing the energy of the herbs as you work.

A Day of Magic
Celebrating the Longest Night

The winter solstice is a time of powerful magic where the sun is at its weakest and the seasons shift from dark to light. It's an auspicious time to go inward and follow any quiet curiosities or intuitive nudges.

In this "in-between" time, you have a chance to slip into another world and change the course of your future. And since it's the darkest point of the year, it's a time where you can see, hear, and begin to incubate exciting new things that have yet to be realized.

Winter's energy is also about conserving—less on action and more on attaining knowledge, learning, and using the quiet moments to explore what might be brewing beneath the surface.

Make the most of the winter solstice by celebrating it all day, from dawn till dusk.

AT SUNRISE: Go outside before dawn and greet the first rays of sunlight. Light a fire or candles to help encourage the sun (since it's at its weakest, it could use your help!). Ring bells and cheer when the first rays of light emerge. Drink hot cider, tea, spiced wine, or wassail, and "pour libations" to the earth as an offering.

AT NOON: Do tarot and divination. Try slow, wintery things like tea leaf-reading or scrying into a glass ornament, fireplace, or candle. Or pull tarot cards and ask questions to find clues to what you want to bring to light next.

AT SUNSET: Time to feast and be merry! Celebrate the sun's light, your own light within, and all of the blessings you've received in this magical year. You made it to the darkest point of the Wheel. Celebrate and welcome back the sun.

Christmas Stockings relate back to a Norse tradition of leaving hay and carrots in boots for Sleipnir, Odin's eight-legged horse. Odin would fill the boots with gifts in return.

Decorative Yule Spellwork
Blessing Your Tree, Log, or Greenery

The winter solstice is the longest night of the year and the shortest, darkest day. Yet it marks the turning point where the days will begin to get longer again—a cause for celebration and anticipation of the sun.

Many Yule traditions involve flames and decorative indoor greenery to herald the return of light and spring. The Yule Log is a well-known custom, where a sanctified and decorated log is burned in the Yule fire. The Yule tree and evergreen boughs represent everlasting life, as they don't wither in winter. They symbolize how we can survive through the dark season. And Scandinavian lore suggests using greenery indoors to give visiting faeries and woodland spirits a warm place for the winter.

As you bring decorative greenery into your home, perform a simple consecration and blessing spell to set the mood and honor it.

You'll Need: A cauldron or incense burner and charcoal to burn frankincense and myrrh. An undecorated Yule log, tree, or altar greenery.

Casting the Spell: Begin by burning the frankincense and myrrh. Circle around your tree or log in a clockwise direction three times. If you can't circle it, you can just stand before it or cast a circle in front of it. Say a few words to thank the spirit of the tree or greenery for its sacrifice to be honored, decorated, and used in ritual for the solstice. Bless it with the power of the elements and then chant the following ancient words, the traditional chant sung when the Yule Log burns on the solstice.

"May the Log Burn, May the Wheel Turn, May Evil Spurn, May the Sun Return."

Scrying With Earth
The Grounding Wisdom of Stones and Bones

As the seasons shift to winter and the element of earth, what do you feel in the depths of your soul? Use any quiet opportunities that arise to slip away and look for wondrous messages to appear from your intuition.

MIRRORS, STONES, & CRYSTAL BALLS
Scrying mirrors are often made of stones like obsidian, which have a black mirror-like finish when polished. They can also be made of glass painted black, of polished metal, or of anything reflective, like a crystal ball.

When scrying into a mirror or ball, gaze at it from an angle so you don't see your reflection. If it's a clear crystal, gaze into its depths. If it's an opaque stone, gaze at its surface. Experiment with using a candle behind or in front of your scrying tool or by wafting herbal smoke for both magical and visual enhancement.

You can also scry with a "regular" mirror and candle in a pitch-dark room. Place the candle between yourself and the mirror. Gaze about eighteen inches away from the mirror, take your time, and look for extraordinary messages to appear in the smoke, in the reflections, and in your consciousness.

RUNE STONES tap into the element of earth as they are commonly made of stones or wooden discs. Rune stones are often cast onto a cloth, and the positions and symbols are divined therein.

THROWING BONES are an otherworldly form of earth divination. The symbolism of the bone sets and techniques used are personal and varied.

And, you can listen literally to the earth. Put your ear to the ground and see what you hear.

Yule Spells

Pink Topaz
Hope & Divinity

The Spirit of Giving
A Spell to Share Magic and Warmth

The festivals and traditions of the winter solstice, the darkest day of the year, have merged from many ancient cultures (a phenomenon called "syncretism") into modern Christmas and neo-pagan Yule.

The practice of giving gifts began as early as the Roman festival of Saturnalia. Ancient people gave in honor of Saturn, the god of agriculture and time, as the sun moves back into Capricorn (ruled by Saturn) on the winter solstice.

Saturnalia gifts were often practical, although outrageous, opulent, or comical items were not uncommon. It was also traditional to write a short, personalized poem with each gift.

TAPERED CANDLES are symbolic gestures of the sun's light. Anoint gift candles with amber oil to signify the sun or cypress for the power of Saturn.

SPOONS & CUPS: Housewares have made nice prezzies for thousands of years. Give ceremonial spoons with painted or wood-burned sigils, or earthy clay cups, bowls, and incense burners.

FOOD: Give a taste of ancient Saturnalia with herbal vinegar, oil, spiced wine, cakes, and cookies.

DOLLS & POPPETS: Make dolls for play or dedicate them to deities or magical workings. Stuff them with symbolic dried herbs and mosses.

STATIONERY and writing implements are just as handy now as they were in 130 BC. Add a drop of perfumed oil or crushed herbs for a magical aura.

A RITUAL OF GIVING: At dawn, pile up the gifts you are giving in the center of the room. Circle around the gifts clockwise, three times, imagining a bright light swirling around the room. Ring bells, sing, and release as much good cheer as you can into the gifts and to the world.

Yule Spells

Simmering Cauldron
A Ritual to Sit in Darkness & Silence

As Yule marks the longest night of the year, there are many ancient traditions to bring brightness, color, and light to the dark of winter, like decorating with shiny ornaments, red berries, and ribbons. You can also use candles and lights to honor the return of the Sun King.

But modern holidays are may feel hectic, so you might like to plan Yule activities that are quiet, reflective, warm, and full of good feelings. It's a poignant time to stop momentarily and let yourself reset and rest in the darkest days of the year. If you'd like to try something chill, this simple Yule ritual can be done alone or in groups.

THINGS YOU'LL NEED: One candle (per person) and matches. The ability to sit in darkness.

For the simmering "cauldron," you'll need a slow-cooker, or you can put a saucepan on your stovetop, or use a real cauldron and hearth fire if you should be so lucky! Then, you'll need water to fill the pot and various herbs. You'll also need to set a timer to check on your cauldron, as you don't want to let it burn dry on your stove. And don't ever leave your simmer pot unattended.

There are some ideas for herbs you can try and some basic measurements on the next page. But feel free to mix and match their magical properties or scents.

DOING THE SPELL: Get your cauldron going with simmering water and herbs. Cast a Circle & Call the Quarters.

Turn off the lights. Sit in darkness and silence. Then, just see what comes to you. What are you feeling in the dark? What does it represent to you, both seasonally and personally? Then light your candle and do the same, seeing what comes, and what the new light represents in your life. Let your candle burn out on its own.

THINGS TO PUT IN YOUR CAULDRON:

Apple: 1/2 cup dried apples or a fresh apple cut into slices for love, healing, and magic.

Bay: 1/2 cup dried bay leaves for protection, healing, and purification.

Cinnamon Sticks: One or two, broken in half. For spiritual enhancement and healing.

Cloves: One tbsp. cloves for protection, wealth, and spiritual enhancement.

Lemon: Use the rind from one lemon or the whole fruit for purification, love, and friendship.

Nutmeg: Add one tbsp. for luck and money.

Orange: Use the rind from one orange or the whole fruit for wealth, love, and luck.

Peppermint: Add 1/2 cup dried peppermint leaves for love, healing, and purification.

Pine: Throw in a handful of pine needles for healing and protection.

Rosemary: Add two handfuls fresh or one cup dried for protection, purification, and healing.

Vanilla: Use 1/2 tsp. vanilla extract to enhance love and the powers of your mind.

Yule Spells

Harmony Charm Bag
A Spell For Holiday Happiness

Even if your family gets along, modern holiday events can be crazy, busy, and stressful. And if you mix in too much togetherness with people that don't get along—parties can feel even more overwhelming.

This year, make a powerful charm bag to bring peace, harmony, and stress-free vibes to the holidays. You can bring it with you if you travel, keep it in your pocket, or hide it in Auntie's house while you are there for the party. You can also tie ribbons around charm bags and hand them out as "sachet" gifts. No relative will resist smelling a lovely sachet that is gifted to them, and they'll also breathe in the calming magical herbs.

YOU'LL NEED: Sachet bags or circles of fabric to tie up with festive ribbons. Herbs and things that symbolize peace, harmony, and stress relief (always use an odd number of items in your charm bag). Here are some ideas: chamomile, clear quartz, fir, gardenia, jasmine, lavender, lilac, mistletoe, peppermint, rose, sage, spruce, St. John's wort, valerian, vervain, and vanilla.

DOING THE SPELL: Cast a Circle and Call the Quarters. Place each item in the bag, visualizing and stating the intention and symbolism. As you tie or sew the bag shut, say the intention to bring holiday harmony and peace to all who welcome and accept it. Consecrate the charm with a drop or two of essential oil or by passing it over a candle flame. Enjoy your holiday!

Yule Procession & Song
Movement & Voice to Honor Tradition

Ancient Yule was a time of song, procession, and communal celebration. People walked from home to home, singing carols and chanting blessings to honor the returning sun.

The music and movement were more than festivity. Songs carried prayers for protection, abundance, and warmth through the longest, darkest nights. Bells rang, voices lifted, and footsteps marked the turning of the wheel.

Have your own Yule procession by caroling with friends and family, or simply by circling around your home or block in silence.

Gather friends, family, or go alone. If desired, light candles or lanterns to carry with you to symbolize the light of the sun. Or carry a bell, or tie ribbons to a walking stick—anything that will flutter and add to the energy of your movement through space and time.

Begin at dusk, walking slowly and letting the sounds of your footsteps be part of the song. If you'd like to sing, choose simple words or traditional Yule carols, or create your own chant that calls for warmth, light, and protection.

As you sing, imagine your voice carrying blessings into the night air, dispersing the energy of your chant. If you're not a singing or noise-making type, let the sounds of the night be the song as you walk by candlelight or darkness. Listen carefully for sounds of birds, owls, creatures, the wind, or merriment from nearby houses.

At the end of your procession, pause and breathe in the night air. Take a moment of silence and gratitude for the endurance of your life throughout the dark seasons.

YULE STARGAZING
EXPERIENCING COSMIC WISDOM AND GUIDANCE

The winter night sky has inspired wonder, guidance, and legends for thousands of years. Stars are messengers, markers of time, and beacons of protection and hope.

In Egyptian lore, the appearance of the star Sirius marked the New Year and was associated with the return of the goddess Isis.

One of the most well-known Christmas stories is that of the Three Wise Men, who followed the brightest star to the Christ child, a legend that celebrates navigation, hope, and the magic of celestial signs.

To experience Yule stargazing, find a quiet, dark space with a clear view of the night sky. Begin by choosing a star to focus on—Sirius, the brightest in the winter sky, is a traditional choice, but any star or constellation that draws your attention will do.

As you watch the stars, breathe deeply, letting your awareness expand outward with the night sky. Sit in quiet awe of the vastness above. Allow your awareness of your human self to fade as you remember that you are a part of it all.

If desired, sit outside for several hours. Watch the slow but undeniable movement of the constellations, noting how they shift from dusk to midnight. Imagine your own life moving in rhythm with these cosmic patterns. See if any wisdom comes to you as your mind clears.

You might like to sketch or paint the night sky or write in a journal, recording which stars you saw, how they made you feel, and the intentions you set beneath them.

At the end of your stargazing, take a final moment to feel your place in the cosmos. Carry the brilliance of the stars into the next few days, remembering that even in the longest night, there is guidance and wisdom available to you.

Reconnect to your instincts by expressing your voice through song or howling at the moon.

Frivolities & the Feast of Fools
Costumes, Games, & Laughter to Make Merry

Merrymaking and goofing off are authentic ways to celebrate the winter solstice, dating back through centuries of folklore, ritual, and communal revelry.

In medieval Europe, the Feast of Fools was a New Year's tradition where commoners wore masks and costumes to invert social hierarchies—singing, dancing, and making mischief dressed as kings, popes, and landlords.

Guising, a practice still alive today, involves traveling from house to house in masks and costumes, singing, telling stories, or performing skits.

These practices helped people to laugh and make-merry in the face of winter's darkness.

To cast your own Yule merrymaking spell, choose or craft a mask that represents an animal or trait you wish to embody or simply a joyful creature that inspires mischief and freedom. Play music that lifts your spirit. Then dance through your house or your neighborhood while chanting, singing, or being silly. Let your costume or mask transform you, embodying a spirit of playfulness and mirth.

If you like, write intentions or blessings on leaves and scatter them, letting the magic of your movement and merriment carry them outward into the world.

Keep your merrymaking mask on your altar through the rest of the season as a reminder that joy, transformation, and celebration are sacred forms of magic—and yours to use.

If you're looking to do something more low-key, watch funny movies, go to a comedy show, see who can do the funniest dance, recall memories that made you laugh, or practice "laughter yoga." All of these practices will bring light and merriment to the dark of winter.

Hearth & Fire
Traditions of Magic & Warmth

Fire is a potent element at Yule, a symbol of warmth, protection, and transformation. In ancient times, the hearth fire was the center of the home. The hearth is a ritual place for casting magic and also a practical place to prepare food and keep warm.

In many European traditions, Yule logs were chosen with great care, then carried into the home as a ritual for health, abundance, and protection. The fire of the Yule Log was not only practical—it was magical, a living presence that connected people to the cycles of the sun.

To practice hearth magic, safely light a Yule log in your fireplace, or drill three holes into a log and place candles within, lighting them ceremoniously. Watch the flames, feel their warmth and energy, and imagine them illuminating the darkness of the long night.

Cast magical herbs into the flames, allowing their smoke to carry your intentions into the air. Roast chestnuts or other symbolic foods over the flames, giving thanks for sustenance and the blessings of the season.

Sit or stand close to the fire and watch the flames dance. Practice divination by noticing shapes, symbols, or messages in the flickering light. Listen to the crackling and popping, hearing the voice of the hearth as it speaks of renewal, endurance, and transformation. You may also chant, hum, or sing songs of protection and gratitude, letting your voice mingle with the fire's energy.

Or simply sit in silence near the warmth of a fire and observe the presence of the fire element and the energy it emits.

After your Yule log burns to ash, keep some of the ashes to use in spells and rituals for protection, purification, and renewal.

Mirrors, candles, and festive lighting will amplify the positive energy of your tarot reading.

Combining garlic, peppers, and onion is a powerful trinity in kitchen witchcraft. Use this trio for protection, cleansing, and amplifying energy.

Yule Kitchen

A Witch's Yule Feast
Kitchen Witchery to Celebrate Your Year

Yule is a feast and celebration of the winter solstice, the longest night of the year and the shortest, darkest day. In alchemy and Hermetic magic, "The End Is the Beginning" is a saying represented by the Ouroboros, a snake eating its own tail, which resonates deeply with the energy of winter's darkness.

PREPARE: Plan a feast! You made it to the darkest point of the year. Celebrate the return of the sun as well as the light within yourself.

Fix whatever food and drink is celebratory for you. Chestnuts and Brussels sprouts are a nice traditional choice, as are roast potatoes, hearty stews, pickles, meat pies, and baked beans. To further set a sacred tone, fill a basket with bread, such as rosemary or herb and olive focaccia. Place dipping bowls of vinegar and oil on the side.

For sweets, gingerbread, peppermints, and truffles are classic choices. Faerie Cakes are an old-timey sugar-and-fruit cupcake that will help you to see the faeries taking refuge in your Yule greens. Chocolate oranges, eggnog, and witchy fruitcake filled with booze-soaked fruit will add to the merriment and signify the coming of spring.

HOLD THE FEAST: Set a table centerpiece or altar with candles, berries, pinecones, evergreen boughs, a Yule Log, or symbols of the sun. Place your feasting foods around it.

Give a prayer or speech, then allow yourself to feel blessed, worthy, and completely supported by the universe and divine spirit for the next twelve holy nights.

Gingerbread Cookie Spell
Kitchen Witchery to Attract What You Desire

Gingerbread is delicious and has been used in spellwork for hundreds of years. Its powers of attraction were commonly known in medieval Europe, where women ate gingerbread men to bewitch themselves and attract a (spicy yet sweet!) husband. And you've likely heard of the witch's gingerbread house in "Hansel and Gretel."

Gingerbread is alluring. When you consider the herbs and spices used in gingerbread, it's no wonder it has such a magnificent quality of attraction. Molasses and ginger are filled with power. Cinnamon brings in connection to divine energy. Allspice and nutmeg will uplift your spirits and vibration. And cloves are a powerful symbol of love and richness of life.

And so, witch up your gingerbread this Yule to attract whatever you desire.

THINGS YOU'LL NEED: Prepare to make gingerbread cookies, including all of the spices above. Use fresh ginger if possible, and consider doubling the amount of spice in your recipe.

PERFORM THE SPELL: Mix up your dough on the solstice. Roll it out and cut it into the shape of what you desire. Use cookie cutters or just a knife. Bake according to your recipe. Decorate using sprinkles and icing of symbolic colors.

State the intention of what you wish. Then repeat the chant above three times while clapping rhythmically at an increasing speed.

Then eat a cookie! Close your eyes. Feel the warmth of the spice drawing in the energy of what you want to attract. Continue to feel good for as many days as you can. Repeat as you are called, until all of the cookies are gone.

Yule Spells

Hearth & Spice
Kitchen Witchery to Stoke Your Flame

The hearth is a symbol of ancestry and the cycle of birth, life, and death.

If your hearth fire went out in ancient Celtic times, misfortune would befall you. People went to great lengths to keep hearth fires stoked.

The Yule kitchen embodies the energy of a fire or hearth deity—the scent of spices, a radiant heat, and an enticing aura of danger that may burst into magical flames at any moment.

In this spell, you'll use the power of spice and light to refresh the energy of your hearth, the undying light of life within your home.

PREPARE by focusing on the things that give light and heat in your kitchen. Clean them all thoroughly. The spice rack, oven, windows, and light fixtures to name a few—hard work, but doing so will yield magical results.

Purchase at least one new spice or refill an old favorite. If you're up to it, create, reorganize, redecorate, or replenish your entire spice cabinet.

Craft an altar in your kitchen, perhaps a clay dish with candles and symbols of deities, fire, and light. Or gather a collection of potent herbs and spices like peppers, onions, garlic, and basil.

RAISE ENERGY: Anoint a spell candle with kitchen magic—roll it in olive oil, then in crushed spices such as cinnamon, rosemary, and thyme.

Light the spell candle at your kitchen altar. Hold your hands to the warmth of the flame while you dedicate yourself to stoking the flames of life within yourself and home.

Commit to "stoking the hearth fire" as a daily ritual either with candles or by eating something with spice and feeling the energy of life within.

Yule Tree Ornaments
Crafty Spellwork and Winter Decorations

The modern celebration of Yule has Norse roots that wove their way into Celtic lore.

With boughs that stay evergreen through the winter, the Yule tree is a symbol of eternal life amid the cycle of the seasons and time. Create ornaments for your tree or evergreen garlands to cast festive magic during Yule's season.

SALT DOUGH: These ornaments are simple with easily accessible recipes and can typically be made with things you've already got on hand (score!). Add herbs or decorate with natural elements such as nuts, seeds, and carved sigils.

WITCH BALLS: The witch balls of yore had string or other small objects stuffed inside to attract evil spirits, spells, and hexes, and trap negative energy within. Create your own witch balls by filling wide-topped ornaments or small jars with herbs, beads, thread, knots of ribbons, or whatever protective elements you like.

WREATHS & GARLANDS: Use ribbon or string to weave a pentacle in the middle of a wreath or tie five cinnamon sticks together into the shape of a star. Try crafting with blackthorn sticks for a brambly dark look. String a festive garland of dried cranberries, orange slices, and popcorn.

RUNES AND SIGILS: Carve or paint runes, oghams, sigils, or other symbols onto small slices of wood or glass balls.

POMANDERS: Stick cloves into a small orange or lemon and let it dry for several weeks. This charm smells wonderful and will bring good luck.

Give the Gift of Witchcraft
Ideas for Crafting Magical Gifts

Yule is the perfect time to craft witchy little gifts. Handmade gifts honor the season's energy of sincerity. It's the perfect opportunity to give your friends and family tangible reminders of the returning light.

Candles are a classic gift: pour beeswax in small molds, adding herbs, spices, or a few drops of essential oil that correspond with your intentions. Decorate with twine, herbal sprigs, dried flowers, or charms.

Soaps infused with herbs and oils make lovely, fragrant gifts. Choose calming scents like chamomile or sweet-smelling combinations like orange and clove. Wrap them in muslin bags with tags describing the herbal magic within.

Fill spell jars with herbs, crystals, or tea blends. Include a note explaining how to perform the ritual or spell.

Scented floor washes and cleaning potions are practical gifts and look super witchy when placed in little jars. Or craft herbal brooms with dried sprigs tied with ribbons—mullein, rosemary, and hyssop are excellent choices.

Beaded jewelry is an elegant way to imbue gifts with crystal magic and intention. Choose colors and stones that reflect the recipient's needs or your shared hopes for the coming year.

Greeting cards can be personalized with hand-drawn symbols, thoughtful poems, pressed herbs, or a light spritz of essential oils.

Cookie kits or baked treats can be paired with instructions for blessing the food or sincere wishes for the recipient's year ahead.

Or give the gift of your psychic sight—bestow your friends and family with gift certificates for tarot or other divination readings.

Yule Cat Greeting Card
Copy onto heavy cardstock. Cut, and mail to your friends.
Finished Size: 4"x6".

About the Artist

Amy Cesari

and her familiars Mr. Toad & Merlin

Amy is an author and illustrator who loves animated musicals. She also likes watercolor painting, witchcraft, and walking on the beach in a really big sun hat.

Not only does she own every Nintendo game console ever made, she's earned several fancy diplomas and enjoys continued studies in various magical practices.

CONTACT AMY AND GET YOURSELF SOME BOOKS & MAGICAL FREEBIES AT:
Amy@ColoringBookofShadows.com
ColoringBookofShadows.com

©2025 Amy Cesari, Book of Shadows LLC

LOVE THIS BOOK?!
THERE'S MORE!

SHOP.COLORINGBOOKOFSHADOWS.COM

Coloring Books:

 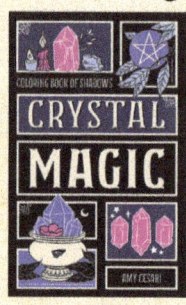  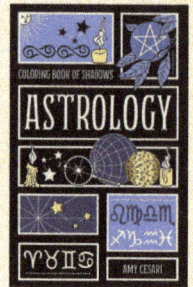

Full-Color Books:

THANK YOU!

Bollank
Art Production

Wendy Ledger
Editor
WendyLedgerAuthor.com

Fiona Horne
Editor of Magick & Editor
FionaHorne.com

Cora Spring Moon
Editor

www.ingramcontent.com/pod-product-compliance
Lightning Source LLC
Chambersburg PA
CBHW050730010526
44107CB00009B/798